The Rescue Task Force

&

Tactical Trauma Care

Manual

for

First Responders

Chief William R. Eppell (Ret.)

Laura J. Kendall, MICP, CPC.

This book contains response and treatment information based on the authors' research of current TCCC & TECC Guidelines, NSC Basic First Aid Guidelines, the Hartford Consensus II, The Report Compiled by Interagency Board: Improving Active Shooter / Hostile Event Response (September 2015), The United States Department of Justice, Federal Bureau of Investigations Study of Active Shooter Incidents in the United States Between 2000 and 2013, Louisiana State University

Activated Threat Integrated Response Training and current best practices.

It is intended to provide information that is helpful and informative. **It does not guarantee a successful outcome or survival should you find yourself, loved one, co-worker, or bystander caught in an attack by an Active Killer.** The authors and all parties mentioned in this book specifically disclaim any and all responsibility for any loss, liability, risks, or consequences which happen directly or indirectly from the use or application of the information contained in this book.

We can all agree that the world has changed over the last two decades. Barely a week goes by without a horrific incident where multiple persons are injured or killed during an Active Killer Event. We have also seen an increase in the number of incidents where first responders are either ambushed or assaulted. As first responders we must all be on high alert and have a greater index of suspicion every time we are dispatched to a call.

It is the simplest dispatch or call that may well turn into the worst call of your life. Our hope is this book will help you have a better understanding of what to look for and how to tactically treat your patients.

As part of the ever-evolving threat matrix, we as first responders must adapt our training, policies and procedures to accomplish our primary mission of protecting and saving lives. This evolution must include at a minimum discussion between police, fire and EMS regarding the Rescue Task Force Concept. As stated in the Hartford Consensus, "It is no longer acceptable for EMS and Fire to stage and wait for casualties to be brought out to the perimeter."

The authors encourage all first responders to attend live, hands-on training courses in your area for Active Shooter and tactical trauma care and continue to attend updated training on a regular basis. It is imperative that you share the training with your co-workers. We must remember that in a time of crisis, we fall back to the level of our training.

Be alert!

Be safe!

Be vigilant!

Train hard!

Go home!!!

Table of Contents

Definitions

AEP: Ambulance Exchange Point

Casualty Collection Point: An area where casualties can be collected and treated. These areas can be located in the Warm Zone, and law enforcement will be assigned to these areas for safety and security.

Citizen First Responder: A layperson who recognizes an emergency and acts to aid.

Cold Zone: An area that is secure from an immediate threat.

Contact Team: A group of law enforcement officers who are assigned the mission to quickly shrink the suspect's area of operation, locate the offender and STOP the offender, arrest or contain   him/her   to   an   area   without   victims.

EMS: Emergency Medical Services

FD: Fire Department

GSW: Gunshot Wound

HOT Zone: Any area where personnel involved in the incident are at extreme risk of death or serious bodily injury due to the actions of a violent offender. It is usually the area where the offender is known or believed to be

ICS: Incident Command System

LE: Law Enforcement

LEO: Law Enforcement Officer

RTA: Rapid Trauma Assessment

RTF: Rescue Task Force

Soft Target: A person or place unprotected/unarmored and vulnerable

Staging Area: An area located in the Cold Zone that is used for organizing and consolidating resources for prior to deployment

Tactical Trauma Care: A specific set of action steps utilized to provide immediate treatment of traumatically injured victims

Triage: The act of sorting victims according to the seriousness of their injuries, as a result of which treatment and transportation decisions are made

Warm Zone: An area believed to be at less risk of harm where the threat is not direct or immediate. The area is at least temporarily secure from the threat, and police officers are present or nearby

Dedication

This book is dedicated to our fellow first responders. By reading this book – and we hope attending a live training course – you are taking the proactive and much-needed step of getting educated on what to do during critical situations, such as an active killer or terrorist attack.

Having knowledge of specific actions to take during an active killing incident may keep you alive to go home at the end of your shift as well as save lives of wounded victims.

Acknowledgements

We would like to acknowledge the following agencies and sites for their invaluable wealth of information on active shootings, workplace violence, and treating the wounded.

The United Stated Department of Homeland Security

The Federal Emergency Management Administration

The ALERRT Center at Texas State University - Creator of Avoid - Deny - Defend

Ready Houston - Run Hide Fight!

The Hartford Consensus II

Interagency Board: Improving Active Shooter / Hostile Event Response (September 2015)

The United States Department of Justice, Federal Bureau of Investigations Study of Active Shooter

Incidents in the United States Between 2000 and 2013

Louisiana State University Activate Threat Integrated Response Training

United States Department of Labor

Occupational Safety and Health and Administration

Officer Survival Solutions

Rapid Application Tourniquets

TECC Guideline (Current as of 2015)

National Safety Council

The Interoperability Board for Local, State and Federal Standardization and Interoperability

C3 Pathways Active Shooter Guide

CBS Interactive Business Network

A special thank you to Samantha Eppell for the cover photo.

Foreword

During my career, I have unfortunately seen what true evil is, and what a sick person or persons can do to other human beings. I have seen the worst in people and numerous unspeakable acts of senseless violence. I have also been fortunate to have seen the best of people in the first responders who routinely respond selflessly and perform incredible acts of bravery on a daily basis to help people. The majority of times, they are understaffed, underequipped, and underappreciated; yet despite that, they routinely perform the impossible. A lot of these situations were so unique that they were not trained or equipped to handle them, but they did the best that they could with what they had (not what they needed), and the majority of the time they successfully completed their mission and saved lives.

The world is changing, and Active Killer events are happening on a regular basis through our country. The time to write the playbook for a response to an Active Killer event is not when it happens; it's before the event. I hope that by reading this book, you will learn some tools that will help you more effectively plan for and handle an Active Killer event.

God Bless You,
Bill Eppell
Founder / Owner WRS Safety, LLC

I've been in the field of EMS since 1981 and a mobile intensive care paramedic since 1986. Not in a million years did I envision the violent and hate-filled world we live in today. Now more than ever, it is important as first responders to educate ourselves on how to survive an Active Shooting or Terrorist Attack and how to provide basic and advanced emergency treatment to the wounded.

Critical incidents such as Active Shooters/Terrorists and workplace violence offenders aren't going away, and I believe it is time to arm ourselves with the knowledge and action steps we need in order to keep ourselves alive and safe, should we be caught in such an event.

Be safe out there and always watch each other's backs!

Peace,
Laura J. Kendall, MICP.
Founder / Owner: Train To Respond, LLC

Live Training & Education Courses

RTFAT: Rescue Task Force Awareness Training

RTF/TTC: Rescue Task Force & Tactical Trauma Care for Police, Fire and EMS. (NJ 7 CEUs)

OSRT: Officer Shot Response Training Course for First Responders. (NJ 3 CEUs)

ASRT: Active Shooter Response Training Course for First Responders. (NJ 4 CEUs)

AKST: Active Killer Survival Training for Civilians. Available for companies, groups, organizations, schools, gun ranges & clubs, places of worship and entertainment venues

RTFTTC: Pre-Test

1. What is an Active Shooter/Killer Event?

   A. Individual(s) actively engaged in killing or attempting to kill people in a confined and populated area

   B. Individuals who enter a building and hurt people

   C. A mentally ill person who is upset

   D. A person who is driven by religious beliefs to injure someone

2. What is a Rescue Task Force?

   A. A team of highly trained medical providers who can provide advanced medical care.

   B. A team of first responders who provide medical support to a SWAT Team

   C. A task force that combines the resources of volunteers from the Fire and EMS Services for immediate deployment at the direction of law enforcement to an Active Shooter / Active Killer incident

   D. All of the above

3. A Rescue Task Force is designed to operate in:

   A. The Hot Zone – an area where there is immediate danger

B. The Cold Zone – an area where little or no danger exists

C. The Warm Zone – an area where danger is possible

D. The Green Zone – an area completely secured by law enforcement

4. In 2014 and 2015, _____ was the fourth leading cause of fatal occupational injuries in the United States

A. Motor Vehicle Accidents

B. Fire

C. Homicide

D. Cancer

5. _____ are concerns for first responders during an Active Killer / Shooter event.

A. Firearms

B. Explosives

C. Knives

D. All of the above

6. Approximately 80% of Active Shooter events are Mass Casualty events.

    A. True

    B. False

7. Venous bleeding is not:

    A. A slow and steady flow

    B. Dark red in color

    C. Blood that spurts out with each beat of the heart

8. When you apply a tourniquet, you should tell the ER staff the following:

    A. Time you placed tourniquet on

    B. Location of tourniquet

    C. Why you applied a tourniquet

    D. All of the above

9. What critical items should be included in an Active Shooter kit:

    A. Tourniquet

    B. Pressure Bandage

    C. Hemostatic gauze or agent

    D. PPE – gloves

E. All of the above

10. All EMS are trained to be in the Warm Zone at an active shooting or stabbing event

11. You can easily spot an arterial bleed even through dark clothing

12. You should keep your active shooter kit with you at all times when on duty

13. A sucking chest wound does not need to be sealed to prevent air going into the chest

14. The majority of Active Shooter/ Active Killer Events last more than 15 minutes

15. Active Shooter/Active Killer events are the sole responsibility of law enforcement.

16. More than 50% of the Active Shooter/Active Killer events have taken place in schools

17. The Rescue Task Force is never allowed to move a patient until a patient assessment has been completed and all injuries have been treated

Chapter One
Active Killers

The purpose of this book is to help give you the knowledge to be able to recognize that a violent event is happening, teach you how to react quickly and appropriately to increase chances of survival, and steps to take to tactically provide trauma care to wounded victims.

Imagine suddenly hearing shots ring out! Would you know what to do? Would you delay acting because you are in denial that an Active Shooting or Terrorist Event is happening?

God forbid you are shot, stabbed or caught in a blast. Would you know how to save your own life? Lately, it seems people can be enjoying a regular day when suddenly mayhem breaks loose as an Active Shooter or Terrorist starts murdering people before their eyes!

Would you know the steps to take to increase your chance of survival if you suddenly found yourself in such an attack? Do you know how to aid victims bleeding from gunshot wounds, penetrating trauma or an explosion?

Our hope is that this book will guide you in what to do in the event you suddenly find yourself trapped in an Active Killer or violent incident, dispatched to one on the job, or are injured with only a precious few minutes to start self-treatment or come to the aid of another who is bleeding out before your eyes.

We hope you can attend a live training course so you can put into practice the action steps and knowledge you will learn in this book. Training is everything in these situations and can literally mean the difference between life and death.

What is an Active Shooter / Active Killer?

Homeland Security describes an Active Shooter/Killer as an individual actively engaged in killing or attempting to kill people in a confined and populated area. In most cases, Active Shooters use firearms, and there is no pattern or method to their selection of victims. Active Shooter situations are unpredictable and evolve quickly.

The FBI definition of a mass shooting requires four or more people killed in one instance (not including the perpetrator).

This leaves out the multitude of other shootings where many people are injured or killed, but four or more people are not killed at one location.

***Mass Shooting Tracker is a site from the GrC community that tracks shootings involving multiple individuals either wounded or killed.

Mass Murderer

One assailant who kills at least four others during a twenty-four-hour period

• 1930 – 1960: Most Active Killers know their target or commit murder during a felony

• 1960 – present: Most Active Killers go for soft targets and shoot unknown bystanders

Active Shooter

An Active Shooter is defined as an individual actively killing or attempting to kill people in a confined and populated area.

- Most use firearms

- No pattern to victim selection

- Pick soft targets with limited security

- They don't go in planning to survive

Active Shooter Profile

Described as:

- Socially isolated

- Harboring feelings of hate and anger

- Often has had some contact with mental health professionals

- Very few have previous criminal records

- Most have had some type of emotional hardship or loss

Terrorism

Terrorist Attacks are happening all over the world with alarming frequency.

Recent Terrorist Attacks with media coverage include: San Bernardino, Paris, Brussels, the horrific attack and murder of Dallas and Baton Rouge police officers and most recently in Las Vegas at the Route 91 Harvest Festival, Orlando at the Pulse Night Club, The London Bridge and The Manchester Arena.

There are many more occurring all over the world and some that do not make the news.

Chapter 1 Quiz

1. According to Homeland Security, an Active Shooter is intent on killing someone they know, i.e., a familiar.

True

False

2. According to The U.S. Department of Labor's Workplace Violence Program, there will be early warning signs of (domestic) violence that is escalating outside the workplace.

True

False

3. First Responders are targets of Terrorist Attacks.
True
False

Chapter 2

Traditional Response Procedures

Traditionally, the most common response procedure throughout the United States during any violent or potentially violent situation is for Fire and EMS to stage outside of the danger area and wait for notification from law enforcement that the scene is safe.

As discussed in Chapter 1, it is not a matter of if there is going to be another Active Killer event, but rather when and where it will occur. In addition to the threat of firearms, we also have to be aware of the other threats such as Improvised or Homemade Explosives, Secondary Explosive Devices, the utilization of fire as a weapon, assaults using knives, edged or impact weapon (such as hammers, etc.) or the use of a vehicle to injure pedestrians.

If an Active Killer event were to happen in your area, what would be the response by your Police, EMS and Fire agencies? Would it be fair to assume that unless there is a change in mindsets, protocol and training, most agencies will follow their standard procedures and stage and wait at a safe location until law enforcement gives the all clear? How long does that take? Are the casualties becoming fatalities while you wait? What are your options?

The Hartford Consensus, which is a joint committee of national experts formed to create a policy to help increase the survivability from Mass Casualty Active Shooter events, states, "The most common cause of preventable death in an active killer mass casualty incident is the failure to control severe bleeding."

We are aware that a casualty with an arterial bleed can bleed out in a few minutes. We also understand that members of the Fire Departments and Emergency Medical Services are reluctant to respond into a known danger area to perform their jobs when a violent suspect is still on the loose. When questioned, they say things like, "It's not our job to get shot at" or "We are not trained to do that." To a certain degree, they are correct. However, we must take into account, who are the casualties in need of our help? In our smaller communities, they are our neighbors, friends and in some cases even our family. But should who the casualties are really matter? They are people who need our help. As first responders, we are trained to identify the problem and immediately come up with a solution with what we have available. So what is the solution to a Mass Casualty involving an Active Killer? What are the options?

Ben Franklin said, **"By failing to prepare, you are preparing to fail."** But how do we prepare to provide lifesaving medical care and evacuate the victims while at the same time providing reasonable protection to our fire and EMS personnel?

Chapter 2 Quiz

1. The response to an Active Killer event is the sole responsibility of law enforcement.

True

False

2. Active Killer events only involve the use of firearms.

True

False

3. The most common cause of preventable death in an Active Killer Mass Casualty incident is the failure to control severe bleeding.

True

False

Chapter 3

The Rescue Task Force Concept

Police, Fire and EMS personnel are well-trained, experienced and equipped to deal with situations that are within their wheelhouse. However, how proficient and comfortable are we in working outside our wheelhouses? How does a police officer, who is not an EMT or paramedic, feel treating multiple trauma victims? How does an EMT, who is not a firefighter, feel inside a burning building? How does a firefighter feel when confronted by an offender armed with a firearm? We would venture to guess that, in all three cases, the answer is "not very comfortable." Every day our first responders do an incredible job of protecting and serving the public.

How and why does this happen? It works because we rely on and trust each other to do what we do best, our jobs. Each profession operates in their "lane" and within their "comfort zone," and all work together to accomplish the mission.

For the most part, when we initially speak to Fire and EMS personnel about the Rescue Task Force concept, they are reluctant to go into an area that has not been made completely secure by law enforcement. So what is the solution? We believe that one of the possible solutions is a Rescue Task force. Before you will be able to get "total buy-in" with the Rescue Task Force concept, you have to educate your first responders. Just as in anything we do, we should understand the statistics of the situations that we face. The FBI and Texas ALERRT reports that 65% of the events are over in less than 5 minutes, 85% are over in less than 10 minutes, and 90% are over in less than 15 minutes.

Is the response to an Active Killer event the sole responsibility of law enforcement? As we talked about earlier, the reason that first responders are so successful in accomplishing their mission every day is that we work together and allow each discipline to do what it does best.

We as first responders are often forced to make the square peg fit into the round hole to accomplish our mission of saving lives. The Rescue Task Force concept is very simple. We all remember from our ICS training that a Task Force is "a combination of resources assembled for a particular tactical need with common communications and a leader." The Rescue Task Force is simply a force multiplier. As we will discuss later, the majority of our police departments will have difficulty in dealing with an Active Killer event that is also a Mass Casualty event.

What if we were to compare two fictional Mass Casualty incidents, the first an Active Killer event with 25 casualties and the second a serious accident on an interstate with 25 casualties, all with the same life-threatening injuries? What is the difference? On the interstate, we rely on the police to ensure that traffic has been controlled and a safe area (Warm Zone) has been established. We enter this Warm Zone and do our jobs because we trust the police to "watch our backs." It's the same philosophy with the Rescue Task Force. Fire and EMS have to trust law enforcement to determine where the Warm Zone is and when it is safe for us to enter. Once we enter the Warm Zone, we have to trust that police will watch our backs, keep us safe as we work and get us safely out when the job is done.

The InterAgency Board on Improving Active Shooter/Hostile Event Response (September 2015) states, "We have to overcome the 'misconception' that an Active Shooter/Killer Event is sole responsibility of law enforcement. It is an all hazards, all responders problem."

The Hartford Consensus II (September 2015) states, "It is no longer acceptable for EMS and Fire to stage and wait for casualties to be brought out to the perimeter."

Does Your Region Need a Rescue Task Force?

The first question all first responders should ask themselves is, if an Active Killer Event with a large number of casualties were to occur in your region, could your local law enforcement effectively handle it by themselves? Do the law enforcement officials in your region have enough officers immediately available to deal with the suspect(s), search for additional suspect(s), and check for additional hazards while employing the proper training and equipment to provide necessary medical care and evacuate the injured to a secure area for transfer to EMS/FD in an acceptable time period?

When law enforcement officers respond to an Active Kill event, their primary mission is to stop the killing. This can be accomplished by a single officer (Contact Officer) or team of officers (Contact Team) entering the area or building and shrinking the suspect's or suspects' operational area, locating the suspect(s) and neutralizing or containing suspect(s) to an area without victims.

The Contact Officer/Contact Teams is not initially concerned with treating the injured because time spent treating the injured while the suspect is still active may result in additional injuries and or deaths. The primary mission of the Contact Teams(s) is to STOP THE DYING.

Over the last decade and a half, law enforcement has been very successful in shifting from the original tactical doctrine of isolating, containing and controlling the scene where an armed suspect was inside and waiting for SWAT and a CNT (Crisis Negotiation Team) to the Rapid Deployment concept. The Rapid Deployment concept involves the immediate deploying of officers into the Hot Zone and neutralizing or containing the threat. Even if the suspect(s) is neutralized very early in the incident, it will still take a considerable time period before the scene is declared safe by law enforcement. During these situations, law enforcement operates on the "Plus One Rule," which means for every suspect they encounter, they must assume there is another suspect still on scene.

If an event occurs in a metropolitan area, there will be a large law enforcement response within a short time period. There will probably be enough staffing to deploy Contact Teams to deal with the threat(s) and deploy Rescue Teams comprised of only law enforcement officers to care for the injured. But what if the incident occurs in a suburban or rural area? In these areas, the law enforcement resources are considerably less and probably take more time to respond in force.

CBS Interactive Business Network reports that 87% of all police departments in the United States have just a few dozen officers. So a department with 36 officers will probably have at most 6 officers on patrol at any given time. Can 6 police officers effectively handle an Active Killer event that is also a mass Casualty incident?

What we do know is that there is a direct relationship between the number of fatalities and the time it takes for the police to neutralize the threat because that time determines how quickly medical care is provided.

If the answer to the question of your local law enforcement agency being capable of handling it alone is no, then we suggest that you explore the concept of a Rescue Task Force with administrators from your local police, fire and EMS.

Chapter 3 Quiz

1. When law enforcement officers respond to an Active Kill event, their primary mission is to stop the killing.

True

False

2. Over 90% of Active Killer Events last more than 30 minutes.

True

False

3. The Contact Officer/Contact Teams is not initially concerned with treating the injured because time spent treating the injured while the suspect is still active may result in additional injuries and or deaths.

True

False

4. During these situations, law enforcement operates on the "Plus One Rule," which means for every suspect they encounter, they must assume there is another suspect still on scene.

True

False

Chapter 4

Rescue Task Force Operations

A Rescue Task Force (RTF) is a force multiplier that combines the resources of personnel from the Fire and EMS Services for immediate deployment at the direction of law enforcement to treat and evacuate Casualties at an Active Killer event.

Sounds simple, but there is more to it than forming an ad hoc task force and running into the danger area. There is no one-size-fits-all Rescue Task Force plan. You have to determine what Rescue Task Force concept is right for your area, considering your resources, geographic makeup and mutual aid capabilities.

The key to implementing a Rescue Task Force is getting the administrators from all disciplines to acknowledge the need for a Rescue Task Force and getting "buy in" from each agency in developing it. The next is the development of policies, tactics, training and equipment for a response to an Active Shooter/Mass Casualty incident. We would highly recommend starting this process by forming a committee of motivated, experienced supervisors / administrators from all disciplines.

You must be cautious not to confuse a Rescue Task Force with that of a Tactical/SWAT Team Medic program. Tactical Medics are highly trained personnel traditionally assigned to SWAT Teams. The initial response to Active Killer Events traditionally falls to patrol officers, not the SWAT Team.

Is your Task Force going to be a made up of responders from a city/town, region, or county? Are you dealing with paid or volunteer personnel or a combination of both? If you plan on developing a regional or county task force, is it covered under your current Mutual Aid Agreements or Memorandums of Understanding, or do these agreements have to be modified?

If you are planning on developing a regional or county-based Rescue Task Force utilizing volunteers, we would suggest that you explore a selection process that includes a physical assessment test, a recommendation procedure where the applicant must be recommended by their agency and a background check. The physical assessment should *not* be based on SEAL team training or the entry physical for a SWAT team but rather an assessment to help ensure that the personnel are fit for the mission. Remember, the mission of the Rescue Task Force is to provide emergency care to the casualties already there, not unintentionally import more casualties.

Tactics

The key to any Rescue Task Force is the use of simple tactics for deployment for the purpose of rapid intervention at the direction of law enforcement to provide medical care to the Casualties in a danger area. We suggest that these tactics be very basic, easy to learn and simple enough that non-law enforcement can quickly become comfortable in using them. We suggest that you consider consistently training in both interior/building and open area operations.

To put it simply: GO-GRAB-GET OUT. GO is deploying the Rescue Task Force into the Warm Zone. GRAB is providing immediate Indirect Threat medical care to the casualties and getting them ready for immediate transport. GET OUT is the swift evacuation of the casualties from the danger area and transfer to EMS.

GO involves the process of marrying law enforcement to the medical portion of the Rescue Task Force and deployment into the Warm Zone to the area(s) where the casualties have been located by the Law Enforcement Contact Team(s). This deployment will only occur at the direction and authorization of law enforcement. Operational frequencies and designated leadership should be established prior to the deployment.

GRAB involves providing immediate lifesaving care and triaging of the casualties. The key to this task is training. This phase of the operation is a whole different process than what your Emergency Medical Providers are used to. This phase involves utilization of Casualty Collection Points and providing Indirect Threat medical care.

Indirect Threat care is basic emergency medical care and involves some very basic skills. If your region has a shortage of Emergency Medical Technicians but has a large number of fire personnel, we recommend that you explore the feasibility of training your fire personnel in Indirect Care.

GET OUT is the process of evacuating the casualties from the Warm Zone/Casualty collection point to the ambulance exchange point and effectively transporting them to appropriate medical care as quickly and efficiently as possible. During this phase, we suggest that you consider using patient movement devices. These devices should be collapsible, easy to use, compact and capable of allowing a single rescuer to move a single Casualty.

The principles of a Rescue Task Force are fairly simple, but the necessary actions are difficult to implement without pre-planning, training and the appropriate equipment.

The most important concepts that must be addressed during any Active Killer event to ensure the casualties receive medical care are Command, Communications and Coordination. The earlier Unified Command and staging area(s) are established, the more effective the operation will be. We recommend utilizing the Active Shooter Checklist by C3 Pathways (http://www.c3pathways.com/asc/) as a guide during an event and during training and policy development.

In order for the response plan to be effective, it must have a clearly defined Area(s) of Responsibility, Area(s) of Operation. To put it simply, who does what where and when. Why recreate the wheel? We recommend keeping it simple: Hot Zone, Warm Zone and Cold Zone.

Hot Zone

The Hot Zone is any area where responders are at high risk of being injured. In general, the Hot Zone is an area where armed suspect(s)/explosives device(s)/threatening device(s) are or are believed to be. Only law enforcement will operate in these area(s).

27

Warm Zone

The Warm Zone is an area that presents less risk to responders. This area is believed to be at least temporarily secure from the presence or movement of anything or anyone that can injure responders. The threat is not immediate or direct, but the potential for incident escalation exists. Rescue Task Forces are permitted to operate in these areas only at the direction of law enforcement and only with a law enforcement security escort. It is recommended that anyone operating within the Warm Zone be equipped with some level of ballistic protection.

Cold Zone

A Cold Zone is a location that is secured from any immediate threat and has been deemed to be safe from any suspect(s)/explosive(s) devices/ threatening devices. Treatment, Triage, Transport and Staging areas, as well as the Command Post, can be established in this area. We caution all first responders not to lull themselves into a false sense of security that any area is really a Cold Zone. Intelligence reveals that suspect(s) plan their attacks well in advance and frequently do pre-event surveillance. Caution should be taken to avoid responding and placing apparatus in the same location every time you respond to a specific location. Intelligence also indicates that suspects reverse engineer the ATF Standoff Distance Recommendation for suspicious devices and will place secondary devices at these standoff distances to kill first responders.

Casualty Collection Point

A Casualty Collection Point and an Ambulance Exchange Point may be located within the Warm Zone.

The Casualty Collection Point (CCP) is a location where the Casualties will receive emergency medical treatment. If located in the Warm Zone, only Indirect Care should be administered. If the CCP is located in the Cold Zone, more detailed emergency medical care can be administered.

If the CCP is located in the Warm Zone, law enforcement will provide either a security escort or establish a security corridor from the CCP to the Ambulance Exchange Point.

The Casualty Collection Point should be established as early as possible in the event. The CCP should be located as close to the casualties as possible, large enough to accommodate the injured and the responders, in a defensible location, and accessible to the Ambulance Exchange Point.

Ambulance Exchange Point

The Ambulance Exchange Point (AEP) is a location where the casualties are transferred from the Casualty Collection Point to a vehicle for transport to a medical facility for definitive care. The AEP can be established in either the Warm or Cold Zones. However, if the AEP is established in the Warm Zone, law enforcement is responsible for providing security for the ambulances both into and out of the Warm Zone. This can be accomplished by law enforcement providing a security corridor or assigning officers as a security bubble for each ambulance.

Incident Command

We don't have to reinvent the wheel here. We recommend utilizing the National Incident Command System (NIMS) or the Incident Command Systems (ICS), which all first responders have already been trained in.

The Incident Commander will be a member of law enforcement, but because of the complexity of Active Killer incidents, Unified Command should be considered. As we discussed previously, we recommend training all of your responders in the 5th Man Concept by C3 Pathways (http://www.c3pathways.com). The 5th Man Concept allows for immediate Command and Control to be established very early in the incident.

There are several different variations on where the Rescue Task Force is placed in the Incident Command Chart. Some have the Rescue Task Force as part of the Law Enforcement Operations Branch, and others have it as part of the Triage Group. This is something you have to decide during your planning process, and whatever you choose should be tested during your drills to see what works best for your area.

The Rescue Task Force Command must work in conjunction with the Law Enforcement, Fire and EMS Commander to successfully manage the incident.

Law enforcement will be the lead agency and responsible for establishing and serving as the Incident Commander. During an

Active Killer Incident, it is imperative that the Rescue Task Force Director/Manager establish Face-to-Face Unified Command with the Law Enforcement Incident Commander as early as possible.

We have participated in numerous Active Killer / Rescue Task Force Drills and found that when Face-to-Face Incident Command was established early during the drill, the operations were more effective.

The Importance of Pre-Planning

One of the most critical tasks that law enforcement must perform early on during an Active Killer event is the mobilization of the appropriate resources as quickly as possible. Decisions need to be made: what resources will be needed? Where should these resources respond? Are there pre-planned staging areas? What agencies will operate on what frequencies? How will these agencies communicate with each other? Is there a command frequency available? What is the plan for diverting the parents or family members who will immediately converge on the scene upon hearing of the event? Are there predetermined locations for reunification? Is there a policy or procedure in place to deal with or prohibit first responders from self-dispatching? Is there a policy in place to minimize unnecessary radio traffic? Is there a plan for transporting the victims who are not injured to a suitable location to be interviewed? Is there a plan to get counselors to a location to begin dealing with the mental health concerns of both the victims and their families? Is there a plan to deal with the press? If so, is it located near the family reunification center?

All of these areas of concern are important and must be considered during an Active Killer Event. However, if you don't have a pre-plan, do you really want to rely on one law enforcement officer or a group of officers to ensure that these areas are quickly addressed? Do you think it is practical to rely on the first responding officers, whose primary mission is to quickly respond to the scene and stop the killing, to at the same time cover all of these additional concerns? Remember what Ben Franklin said, "By failing to plan, we are preparing to fail." We must discuss all of these areas before an event with all agencies that will be involved and come up with a plan. We have seen time after time that we may have great pre-plans for certain events, but the "boots on the ground" have never seen them. Once you come up with a plan, you must test it by drilling on it, identifying its deficiencies and then addressing the deficiencies by revising the plan. Deficiencies will usually fall into three areas: a Deficient Plan, Training Issues or Personnel Issues.

Direct Threat Care

Direct Threat Care is the type of care that can be administered in the Hot Zone and involves direct pressure and tourniquet application for bleeding control and placing the casualty into the recovery position.

Only law enforcement officers will operate in the Hot Zone.

It is import to instruct your responder that the first option for Direct Threat Care is to determine if the casualty can self-evacuate to a safer area and provide self-aid. If the casualty cannot self-evacuate, then a decision has to be made as to whether the rescuer can safely get to the casualty and render aid. If the situation is too dangerous to accomplish this, law enforcement must change the situation by neutralizing the threat or moving (pushing) the threat out of the area.

Indirect Threat Care

Indirect Threat Care is the type of care that is provided by either the Rescue Team, which is comprised of only law enforcement officers, or the Rescue Task Force. Indirect Threat Care is performed in the Warm Zone and involves the use of direct pressure, hemostatic agents, pressure bandages, tourniquets, nasal pharyngeal airways, chest seals, and treating for hypothermia. Depending on the level of training and state regulations, Indirect Threat Care can also involve needle decompression and IV/IO therapy.

Triage

What is triage? Is it an art or a science? "Triage is defined as the process of determining the priority of treatment based on the severity of condition." How proficient are all of our first responders in triage? Is this an area that we frequently train in?

During an Active Killer event, law enforcement operates under the SIM principal: **S**ecurity, **I**mmediate Action and **M**edical. Law enforcement contact teams are trained to enter a room, dominate it, address any immediate threat and identify casualties. The medical portion of this phase involves law enforcement conducting a quick and modified form of triage that involves utilization of three categories: Red, Green and Uninjured. An example of this type of Direct Threat Triage involves law enforcement giving verbal commands to the victims such as "If you can hear my voice, move to the back wall." This group is then given another command such as "If you are uninjured move to the side wall." The victims who moved to the side wall are classified as Uninjured. The victims that moved to the back wall and remain there are triaged as Green, and the victims who do not or cannot move are triaged as Red. This vital triage information and location must be immediately relayed to the Incident Commander.

The Law Enforcement Rescue Team and the Rescue Task Force should be trained to utilize the traditional triage consisting of Black, Red, Yellow and Green. We recommend utilizing triage ribbon instead of the traditional triage tags during this phase of the operation.

We frequently use casualty cards during training, which are laminated cards that give a casualty description (age, gender, etc.), signs, symptoms and vital signs. A responder is given a card and has to place the casualty into a triage category. We have frequently seen variations in the triage level for the same casualty. An example is a 35-year-old police officer who was shot in the left arm and had an arterial bleed with moderate blood loss. The officer had self-applied a tourniquet and is conscious, alert and able to walk. In what category of triage would you place this casualty? We have seen this casualty triaged as Green, Yellow and Red.

The key to effective triage is training. Proper triage at an Active Killer – Mass Casualty event is very important and it is imperative that we do our best to get it right. We have seen during numerous exercises that the responders give boilerplate answers for a perfect world and not the situation that they are in.

During our training classes, we will have one responder enter a room with four or five seriously injured casualties in each corner of the room. It is very common to see this sole responder run from corner to corner treating and triaging the casualties. The responder can be quickly overwhelmed, and we have even seen a few of them "shut down." The key to effectively handle this situation is to consolidate the victims as close together as possible. This allows for more effective casualty management and minimizes some of the physical stress for the responder.

Chapter 4 Quiz

1. A Rescue Task Force (RTF) is a force multiplier that combines the resources of personnel from the Fire and EMS Services for immediate deployment at the direction of law enforcement to treat and evacuate Casualties at an Active Killer event.

    True

    False

2. A Rescue Task Force member and a SWAT Team Tactical Medic have the same level of training.

    True

    False

3. The _____ Zone is any area where responders are at a high risk of being injured. In general, the _____ Zone is an area where armed suspect(s)/explosives device(s)/threatening device(s) are or are believed to be.

A. Warm Zone

B. Cold Zone

C. Hot Zone

D. Yellow Zone

4. The _____ Zone is an area that presents less risk to responders. This area is at least temporarily secure from the presence or movement of anything or anyone that can injure responders. The threat is not immediate or direct, but the potential for incident escalation exists.

A. Warm Zone

B. Cold Zone

C. Hot Zone

D. Danger Zone

5. The Casualty Collection Point should be established as early as possible in the event. The CCP should be located as close to the casualties as possible, large enough to accommodate the injured and the responders, in a defensible location, and accessible to Ambulance Exchange Point.

True

False

Chapter 5

Surviving an Active Killer Event

Tips to Surviving an Active Shooting

The most important thing you can do to help avoid becoming a victim of violent crime is to exercise "Situational Awareness," which is simply always being aware of your surroundings. The next biggest key to survival is recognizing that it is going down, and you are caught in an Active Shooting/Killer event, act of workplace violence or Terrorist Attack. There are numerous accounts from victims who were present during an Active Killer event and made statements to the effect of "I was doing my job and I thought I heard gunshots. I then continued to do my job..." Don't deny that something bad is happening!!!

He or she who hesitates is lost - literally!

The following training sites and videos are ones we use to both educate ourselves and teach Active Shooter Response & Tactical Trauma Care Courses. For those of you who are unable to attend a training course, we have included the site links so you can go directly there and learn more.

According to the U.S. Department of Homeland Security's *Active Shooter – How To Respond and Ready Houston – Run Hide Fight,* there are three things you can do if caught in an active shooter situation.

1. Run!

Not blindly, but with a plan!!

1. Know your route. Plan it ahead!

2. Remember, in a large building, gunshots can be deceiving. You can actually be running towards the shooter when you think you are running away. If you are unsure where the shots are coming from, consider hiding (Avoiding).

3. Leave your stuff behind. Stuff does not save lives!

4. Help others get out!

5. Stop others from heading towards the Active Shooter/Killer! Keep your arms in the air and make sure that there is nothing in your hands – like you are surrendering with your hand opened and fingers spread apart. Your hands should be between your shoulders and head as you run out. This will help prevent you and your kids from getting accidentally shot by responding law enforcement.

6. Follow the instructions of law enforcement.

2. Hide (Deny)

The simple act of getting yourself behind a locked door can increase your chances of survival. If at all possible, consider using the Barricade Plus concept, by placing additional obstacles such as tables, chairs etc. in front of the door. Hiding and Hoping is not a strategy. Hiding (denying) with a plan to defend yourself is. You also must have a plan if the suspect(s) manages to gain entry into the room, and that plan is defending yourself.

Cover vs. Concealment

In an active shooter situation, one of the things to think about is "What can I hide behind?" There are two types of places to consider.

Cover is an object or objects that are likely to stop bullets. This not only helps you from being seen, but also will protect you from bullets. Most obvious types of cover are cement walls, vehicles (engine area), steel doors, etc.

Concealment is basically not being seen. Concealment offers no ballistic protection. Examples of concealment are sheetrock and plywood walls, desks, vehicle doors, tinted glass, and bushes, etc. In an Active Shooter situation it is important to know if you are using cover or concealment. An excellent mental exercise we do when in a building or a public place is to look for areas of cover and/or concealment as well as primary and secondary exit points. When selecting cover, determining the type of firearm used will make a difference in assessing how much protection the cover will provide. This can be as simple as determining if the suspect(s) are using handguns or long guns (assault weapon, rifle or shotgun). As a general rule, long guns have a longer range than handguns.

Knowing where you are moving to before you leave is important as well. Have a plan before you start to move! This is why it is important to familiarize yourself with your surroundings. Knowing which direction windows open and what level in a building you occupy is essential. Remember to consider alternate exit points such as windows and hatchways. This information is also important to let other responders know where you are and what you are reporting!

3. Fight – last resort only!
<u>Fighting as a last resort!</u>

Historically, Active Shooters do not like confrontations. The new breed of Terrorists, however, have the main purpose of killing and wounding as many as possible. We are not advocating purposely putting yourself in harm's way, but sometimes there is no other choice but to defend yourself. You have a right to defend yourself!

Acquiring some self-defense skills before having to defend yourself is obviously a good idea. The time and money used to take basic martial arts training or pepper spray training can be a lifesaver.

Let us reiterate that you have a right to defend yourself if you are being attacked and your life is in danger.

It is extremely important that you mentally prepare yourself to do whatever it takes to survive the incident. You must know your ability, your strengths and limitations. It is imperative that you think about having to defend yourself before an incident. This is called "Spinal Tuning." You must have the mindset that you are in a fight for your life and you are going to win this fight. You are going home to see the people that you love.

Don't fight fair! Your attacker isn't fighting fair and wants you dead!

In our live and online training courses we focus mainly **on Avoid - Deny - Defend** as the way to survive an active shooting.

At the ALERRT Center in Texas State University they examined these choices(run, hide, fight) even further and found another way of reacting to an active killer situation.

They found three things you can do that have proven effective if caught in an Active Killer situation. What you do matters!!

You have 3 choices:

1. Avoid!

2. Deny!!

3. Defend!!!- You have a right to defend yourself!!

According to the ALERRT Center - Avoid - Deny - Defend the first step starts with your state of mind.

AVOID

1. Situational Awareness - be aware of what is going on around you.

2. Have an exit plan. (Know your exits not just the door you came into.)

3. Move away from the threat as quickly as possible.

4. The more distance and barriers between you and the threat or shooter increase survival.

DENY

When it is difficult or impossible to get away from the threat you must deny!

1. Keep distance between you and the threat/shooter.

2. Create barriers to prevent or slow down a threat /shooter from getting to you

3. Turn the lights off. and silence your phone or other devices.

4. Remain out of sight and quiet by hiding behind large objects.

5. Lock the doors.

6. Be ready to react if the threat gains entry.

DEFEND

If you can't get way for the threat/shooter or deny then you must be prepared to fight and defend yourself.

You have the right to survive!

I'll talk a little about mindset here. Mindset is everything in these type of attacks. You must have the mindset that "I AM GOING TO SURVIVE!"

1. Be aggressive and committed to your actions!

2. Don't fight fair!

3. You have the right to survive! You are fighting for your life!

You can learn more at <u>avoiddenydefend.org</u>

Survive /Self Aid

In addition to the concepts of Run/Hide/Fight or Avoid/Deny/Defend, we encourage you to train yourself to provide first aid to yourself and possibly others (Self Aid /Buddy Aid), which we will describe in Chapter 6.

If you suddenly find yourself in a situation where someone is shooting at you, what physiological reactions will happen to you? Will your respirations increase? Will your heart rate also increase? Unless you are under the influence of drugs or alcohol, the answer will be YES. As a result of the increase in your heart rate, some catastrophic things will start happening in your body. You might experience: narrowed vision, diminished hearing, reduced fine motor skills, inability to speak or difficulty speaking, and diminished cognition. So when your heart rate goes really high, you will have problems seeing, hearing, talking, dialing a phone and thinking. All of which you will need to help you survive.

So what can you do to quickly lower your pulse to help you survive? It's simple: Tactical Breathing. Take slow deep breaths, 5 seconds in, hold for 5 seconds and exhale for 5 seconds. It was originally called Lamaze Breathing and is used during childbirth. We call it tactical breathing because it sounds cooler.

So simply by breathing, you will be able to think more clearly, and this will drastically increase your chances of surviving the incident.

Chapter 5 Quiz

1. List the three things that Texas State University says have proven effective in surviving an active shooting.

    A.

    B.

    C.

2. You should grab all your stuff before exiting during an active shooting.

    True

    False

3. Provide the best definition for the following:

Cover:

Concealment:

Chapter Six

Now we will start digging deep into the aftermath of an Active Shooting. Here we will learn how you can help yourself or other victims of a shooting or penetrating traumatic injury such as a stabbing.

Gunshot Wounds

It is imperative, after a shooting, that you check the victim or yourself not only for an entrance wound but an exit wound.

*Entrance wounds tend to be smaller.

**Exit wounds can be huge blow-out wounds.

You must treat both if there is an arterial bleed.

***Sometimes the bullet stays inside the body and there is no exit wound.

Rapid Trauma Assessment (RTA)

Law Enforcement will enter the Hot Zone with the single goal of neutralizing the shooter. Once the shooter is neutralized, they will aid victims. Until then, if you are trapped in an Active Shooting or Attack, you will be on your own and may be the first one to render aid to the victims or perform self aid.

This is rapidly changing, but right now most of us, as EMS providers, are not trained or properly outfitted with ballistic gear to enter the Warm Zone!

However, if you and your agency are properly trained and outfitted with ballistic gear, most likely you will be directed into the Warm Zone (where there is a chance you could be shot). If you are not trained, you will be in a staging area until the scene is declared safe by PD.

➡Be alert and follow law enforcement directions.

Non law enforcement first responders, the first question you need to ask yourself as you arrive at an Active Killing is, "Is the scene safe?"

If the scene is not safe and you could be shot or killed, do not attempt rescue or treatment unless trained specifically for such an event.

Your safety comes first! Always!!

There have been instances where Active Killers / Terrorists attempt to get away by pretending to be a victim! When assessing, be on high alert for a weapon! You are not just looking for injuries at these scenes, but weapons of any kind on your patients!

There are two categories of emergency first aid in an Active Killer situation.

Self aid: Treatment you do to save your own life.

Buddy Aid: Treatment you do to save another person's life. (This may include instructing others in how to aid themselves if you are unable to reach them.)

Rapid Trauma Assessment

When you come upon an injured or shot person, the first thing you will do is a rapid assessment for life-threatening injuries.

Check: Are they conscious? Can they speak?

Check: Do they have a pulse? Are they breathing?

- Check radial artery. If they have a radial, this tells us they have a blood pressure.

- If you can't feel the radial pulse, then check the carotid artery.

If there is no pulse and there are enough rescuers to help all critical victims, then start CPR.

If the victim has a pulse and is breathing, then check for bleeding.

Basic Bleeding Interventions

1. **Recognize it.** Don't let dark uniforms or clothing cause you to miss this deadly injury. Look for pooling blood around the victim, clots and wet or dark areas on the clothing.

2. **Apply gloves** to protect yourself against blood-borne diseases.

3. **Apply direct pressure** by holding a dressing or something clean over the wound and press down hard.

If bleeding doesn't stop, you can **elevate the extremity if there is no fracture present or gross deformity of the limb.**

Don't freeze at the sight of blood or injuries, which can be horrific – our goal as first responders is to *stop the bleeding!*

Triage

If there are multiple victims and not enough rescuers, then triage must come into play.

As hard as it may be to do if there are more victims than rescuers, you must move on to the one you can still try to save. One who is still alive but may be bleeding out takes priority.

Chapter 6 Quiz

1. There will always be an exit wound in a shooting victim.

   True

   False

2. RTA stands for?

   A. Run Tourniquet Artery

   B. Rapid Trauma Assessment

   C. Rubber Tourniquet Application

   D. Rapid Tourniquet Application.

3. You will easily be able to spot bleeding.

   True

   False

Chapter Seven

Bleeding

Three types of bleeding:

Capillary Bleeding

Capillaries are the smallest blood vessels in the body. They deliver oxygenated blood to the tissues and take back deoxygenated blood to the veins. Capillary bleeding is slow and oozes out. It stops quickly with direct pressure.

Venous Bleeding

Veins carry blood with little to no oxygen in them which explains the dark red color. They are not under pressure and bleed slow and steadily.

Deep lacerations have the potential to cut open veins.

The best way to stop most cases of venous bleeding is to put direct pressure on the wound.

This is when a Pressure Bandage would be applied to help slow and stop the bleeding.

But remember we don't want to stop the pulse in the affected area, so not too tight!

Arterial Bleeding – the Killer!

Arteries carry freshly oxygenated blood (which is why arteries have bright red blood in them) from the heart to be distributed to the tissues of the body. Because they carry rich oxygenated blood that must go throughout the body, they are under pressure. This is why arterial bleeds are so deadly.

Arterial bleeding is the least common but most deadly type of bleeding. In an arterial bleed, the blood **is bright red and spurts out each time the heart beats. Picture a garden hose at full blast. This is what a bleed of a major artery looks like. The victim will be dead in 3 - 5 minutes if no first aid is given.**

In most cases of arterial bleeding, direct and extremely firm pressure on the wound is the best way of stopping it.

If direct pressure is not applied, a severe arterial wound can cause you to bleed to death within a few minutes.

Arterial bleeding may be hard to notice right away if the victim is wearing dark clothing or if the environment is dark. You will need to look at the clothing and watch for pooling of blood in one spot that seeps through the clothing.

Treat fast - the victim can bleed out in 3-5 minutes!

If you have attempted to control the bleeding with direct pressure, and it will not stop, you must immediately apply a tourniquet to stop the bleeding.

Here are some things to remember:

1. Tourniquets are for massive bleeding and control.

2. Never apply a tourniquet over a wound.

3. Only use them on extremities.

4. Write down the time of application for other responding EMS or the receiving hospital.

5. Once applied, it stays on – DO NOT REMOVE.

<u>Tourniquets should be used to control massive bleeding that cannot be stopped with direct pressure.</u>

The benefit of tourniquet use in patients with massive hemorrhage has been proven and is now the standard of care.

Advanced Bleeding Care Techniques & Equipment

Police Statistics

Two-thirds of all preventable police officer deaths are due to severe hemorrhaging, caused by penetrating trauma injuries such as arterial gunshot wounds.

The ability to reach wounded officers or victims or start self aid within moments of injury, especially penetrating traumatic injuries, can mean the difference between life and death.

These statistics are for police officers but apply just as much to any victim of a shooting or stabbing.

*If you do not start self-treatment or treatment of a victim with an arterial bleed from a gunshot, stab wound or other mechanism, death will occur within 3- 5 minutes!

*Depending on the wound, in as little as 20 seconds you will experience loss of fine motor skills and diminished

consciousness – Get off the "X" and get a CAT on within 20 seconds. The "X" is the locations where you were assaulted and are still vulnerable.

That's why keeping a gunshot /trauma pack on your person is so critical.

Trauma **Kits**

There are many different types of trauma kits specifically designed for severe arterial bleeding.

Wherever you get your kit, it should contain the following at a minimum.

1. Personal Protective Equipment – Gloves.

2. Tourniquet (Swat T, RAT, CAT).

3. Hemostatic Gauze.

4. Chest Seals

5. Pressure Bandage.

Each piece of equipment is vitally important in treating a severely injured shooting victim with an arterial bleed. We will go over in depth how to utilize each piece of equipment.

Using a Trauma Kit

The initial rapid trauma assessment of an injured victim will help you determine what is needed and how you will treat them.

Keep them calm and reassure them because the faster the heart beats, the more blood loss there is.

RTA should take only seconds. Conduct a head-to-toe exam; quickly, with the main goal being to find all major life threats.

Remember to always check for an exit wound on the victim. Don't skip it; this could be deadly.

Tourniquet Do's & Don'ts

Remember Tourniquets are for extremities ONLY

1.Place the tourniquet above the affected joint. Never over top of a joint! (Joints in the arm are the wrist, elbow, shoulder. Joints in the leg are ankle, knee, hip.)

2. High & Tight! Apply the tourniquet 3 - 6 inches above the wound and never over top of the wound!

3. Tighten until bleeding stops and there is no distal pulse.

4. Tell EMS or the hospital there is a tourniquet on the victim you are with.

Types of Tourniquets

CAT - Combat Application Tourniquet

A CAT is a truly effective tool that when used correctly stops bleeding in extremities. The CAT is patented and can be applied using one hand.

Image courtesy of North American Rescue

To learn more go to North American Rescue https://www.narescue.com/

To join our online Bleed Control Specialist Training go to traintorespond.mykajabi.com

RAT - Rapid Application Tourniquet

Rats Medical defines the RAT as: ?R.A.T.S – *Rapid Application Tourniquet* – A solid vulcanized rubber core with a nylon sheath combined with a unique locking mechanism make this a simple and incredibly fast *tourniquet* to *apply* to self or others. The RATS hallmark is use under stress.

U.S. PAT. NO. 9,168,044

Image courtesy of Rats Medical

To learn more go to Rat's Medical

https://ratsmedical.com/

Action Steps for Applying a Swat T Tourniquet

1. Place the tourniquet above the affected joint. (3 - 6 inches above wound if possible.) Never over the top of the wound!

2. Secure tourniquet.

3. Never leave the victim unattended when a tourniquet is applied. Tell other EMS or the hospital there is a tourniquet on the patient when you are transferring care.

4. Document the time of application, why you applied it, and where it is on the body.

.

Using a Swat T tourniquet step by step

Deploy SWAT-T Tourniquet and Stretch it tight. Wrap it 6 inches above the wound if possible.

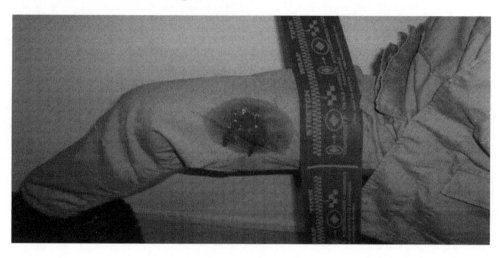

Continue the wrapping process to ensure tightness with each wrap.

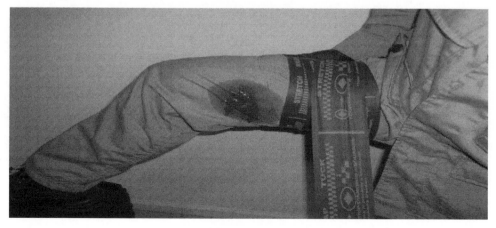

As you come to the last few inches, tuck the end of the tourniquet inside the wrap to secure it.

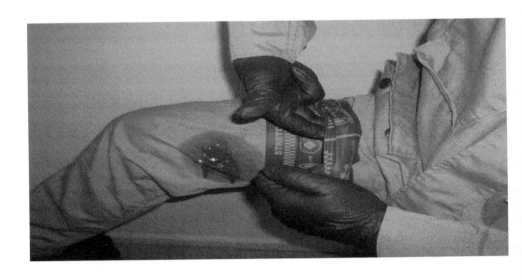

SWT: Stretch, Wrap and Tuck Tourniquet.

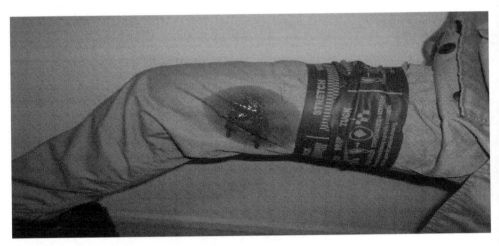

Images courtesy of Officer Survival Solutions.

Hemostatic Gauze

Hemostatic Gauze is a chemical agent that stops bleeding. There are several different kinds. If you are EMS, Fire or Police, remember: **It must be approved for use in your state and by your agency.**

Hemostatic Gauze is used when direct pressure and an applied tourniquet do not stop the hemorrhaging, or the injury is in an area where you cannot apply a tourniquet, such as the neck.

➡It is important to be trained in the use of hemostatic gauze and feel confident in your ability to use it properly and when needed.

Step 1: Tear open Hemostatic Gauze pouch at the indicated tear notches and take out the Hemostatic Gauze.

Step 2: Pack the Hemostatic Gauze all the way down into the wound cavity until you make contact with the severed or torn artery.

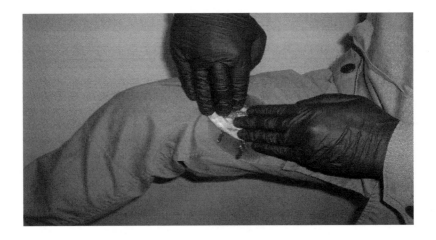

Step 3: Immediately apply direct pressure and hold that pressure for at least 3 minutes.

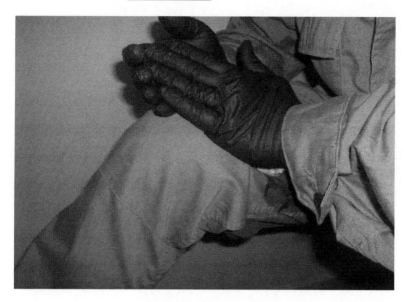

Applying the Pressure Bandage

Step 1: Apply the Emergency Pressure Bandage with non-stick pad directly over the wound.

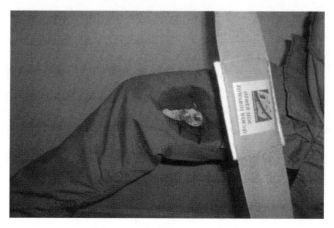

Step 2: Wrap tightly, creating pressure to be forced down onto the wound.

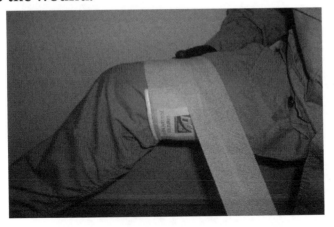

Images courtesy of Officer Survival Solutions.

Chapter 7 Quiz

1. Two-thirds of all preventable police officer deaths are due to severe hemorrhaging caused by penetrating traumatic injuries such as an arterial gunshot wound.

    True

    False

2. You will bleed to death in _____ from an arterial bleed?

    A. 5 - 8 minutes.

    B. 1 minute.

    C. 3 - 5 minutes.

3. In a gunshot victim, immediately apply a tourniquet, even if bleeding stops with firm direct pressure.

    True

    False

4. Venous bleeding is a deadly killer.

True

False

5. Tourniquets are not

A. Used only on extremities.

B. Used for massive arterial bleeding control.

C. Applied to all gunshot victims even if direct pressure has stopped the bleeding.

6. When using Hemostatic Gauze, place it lightly on the surface of the wound.

True

False

Chapter Eight

Traumatic Injuries

Obvious penetrating chest wound from bullet, knife, or other object.

GSW or stab wound to the chest area.

** Not only may vital organs be damaged, but air is now going in through the chest hole.

** Air from mouth/nose and the open hole in chest fills the chest cavity. This causes compression of the lungs and vital organs.

Immediate goal is to seal the chest wound!

** Remember to check for an exit wound.

** Sucking Chest Wounds: Make sucking noise as air goes in and out, and frothy blood may be coming from the hole. Air always follows path of least resistance.

* Victim experiences extreme shortness of breath and rapid heart rate.

* Lungs may collapse.

* Without treatment, they will die.

Treatment

Step 1: Expose chest.

Step 2: Look for entrance and exit wound. Seal both.

Step 3: If object is impaled such as a knife – leave it in and secure it in place. The object may be compressing an artery so if you pull it out, the artery will burst open and the victim will bleed to death.

Step 4: On exhalation Cover the open chest wound with a vented chest seal. If a vented chest seal is not available, a non-vented one can be used.

** When the victim exhales, the air leaves the chest. That is the best time to apply the seal.

** Chest seals prevent air from going in through the GSW/open wound in the chest.

85

Remember!

*** Monitor the victim frequently. If their breathing worsens, you may have to "burp the seal" (lift up one end of the seal as the patient exhales and then reseal) or allow air out through the valve in the chest seal.

Blast Injuries

Blasts, such as those from a Terrorist/Suicide Bomber, cause massive injuries and deaths. The injuries can be very disturbing when you see them.

Injuries commonly seen with blasts are:

Traumatic amputations

Massive Bleeding

Impaled objects

Burns

Shock

What can you do if caught in a bombing?

1. Approach the blast scene with your safety in mind!

2. There may be secondary devices!!! Plan on it!! In fact, it is better to go in knowing there will be secondary devices. Keep your eyes and senses open! NO TUNNEL VISION!

3. Report any suspicious devices immediately and use caution utilizing a radio or cellphone near a device.

4. Keep a safe distance from any suspicious device. Remember, if you can see the device, the device can kill you.

5. Utilize the ATF's Bomb Threat Stand Off Chart (*https://www.atf.gov/explosives/table-distances*)

Scene size-up

<u>How many people are injured?</u>

<u>What are their injuries?</u>

<u>Is there a chemical component? (chemical warfare) –</u>
Hazmat!

Remember

➡It will be mass chaos – be prepared.

➡Our job as first responders is to begin sorting the victims according to how seriously they are injured and start treating!
Walking wounded: get them out of the scene. Let them self-extricate if possible, but remember active shooters and terrorists have been known to masquerade as victims. Keep a high index of suspicion with all victims you are assessing and treating.
If the walking wounded are self-extricating from the scene, instruct them where to go.

Traumatic Amputations

Traumatic amputations – control massive bleeding!

Do an RTA – find life-threatening injuries or problems.

1. Apply direct pressure.

2. If bleeding does not stop, apply a tourniquet.

3. Treat for shock.

4. Recover the amputated part if possible.

Preserve the amputated part by wrapping it in sterile saline-soaked gauze and place it in a watertight container or resealable plastic bag. Place the protected part in container with ice. Do not allow the damaged part to come in direct contact with ice.

In a blast injury, the limb or parts may be too badly damaged to recover or preserve.

Impaled Objects

Many explosive devices have been loaded with shrapnel, which upon detonation will impale the victims. Likewise, ordinary objects caught up in the blast wave can impale victims.

Perform an RTA to find life-threatening injuries or problems.

1. Treat life-threatening problems or injuries immediately.

2. Leave impaled object in and stabilize it.

3. If the object is large, such as a fence, it may require extrication/cutting.

4. Treat major bleeding.

Burns

Blasts/bombs can cause burns in a significant number of victims. The hot gases from the blast wave start burning the victims as soon as it makes contact with them.

Burns can be devastating to look at and may be what initially grabs your attention, but you MUST be on alert for traumatic injuries the victim has sustained and treat them as well!

Burn Treatment

Do an RTA to find life-threatening problem or injuries.

1. Look for soot and singeing of the hairs in the nose, eyebrows, beard, head, and look in the mouth for swelling or redness. (Do not probe into the mouth as it can cause massive swelling and cut off the patient's airway!)

2. Burns to the face = burns to the upper airway = <u>swelling!</u>

Basic interventions: Manage airway by oxygenation and ventilation.

Advanced interventions may include: RSI, Intubation, Trach.

3. Stop the burn process. (Follow your local protocols.)
Remove the victim from the heat source.

***If burned area is greater than 20% of the body, do not **saturate the victim with water – you do not want to cause hypothermia!**

Leave blisters intact.

Act quickly to prevent heat loss and hypothermia.

Apply dry sterile dressing/sheets over the patient as well as under the patient if possible.

Transportation Decisions

What type of hospital should victims go to and why?

A. Victims will be transported to a burn center unless there are traumatic injuries.

B. **Burn victims with traumatic injuries go to a trauma center first.**

Traumatic injuries always get treated first at a trauma center.

Vehicle Attacks

Warnings have gone out from authorities that Vehicle-Ramming Attacks by Terrorists are increasing in frequency.

We need only to look at the statistics for 2016 and 2017.

Studies cite that vulnerable locations include anywhere there will be a large gathering of people.

-Sporting events

-Malls

-Entertainment venues

-Parades

-Celebratory gatherings

You must have situational awareness at all times when at a location with large gatherings of people.

In July 2016 in Nice, France, a Vehicle Attack using a large truck killed 86 people and wounded 434, and since then there have been many more Vehicle Attacks around the world.

At a Vehicle Attack as with a large scale Active Killer attack you must expect a chaotic scene with multiple fatalities and multisystem traumatic injuries.

Be alert for multi-pronged attacks! In many of the latest attacks in the US and UK, the first attack is by Vehicle, and then the Active Killer leaves the Vehicle and begins shooting or stabbing victims.

Situational Awareness is KEY!

If you see or get dispatched for a vehicle crash into a crowd – approach with thoughts of a terror attack in your mind. Do not become a victim of the secondary attack.

Scene Safety

To provide basic aid to victims of a Vehicle Attack or any attack by an Active Killer you must first make sure the scene is safe.

***You do not want to become another victim.

Be alert and have situational awareness. No tunnel vision!

Until the police neutralize the Active Killer, the scene will be dynamic, unsafe and ever-changing.

Emergency First Aid

If you find yourself caught in a Vehicle Attack:

Can you get yourself and others to a place of relative safety?

-Perform a rapid trauma assessment to find life threats.

No Pulse. Note: current guidelines recommend performing CPR only if it is safe to do so and the Active Killer/s have been neutralized (Cold Zone).

-Stop bleeding with direct pressure, tourniquets, hemostatic gauze and pressure bandages.

-Keep the victim from moving, especially if you suspect a spinal cord injury.

-Keep the victim warm until you are able to affect transport. It is now being found that many victims are dying from hypothermia, so keeping them as warm as possible is important.

-Comfort them. We believe that hearing is the last sense to go. We always talk to our unconscious or severely injured patients, speaking words of comfort and explaining everything we are doing.

In these horrific situations, sometimes this is all we can do for our patients who are badly injured or dying.

We believe it is one of the most important things we have done and continue to do in our first-responder careers.

Positioning of Victims

Because every situation is different, and we can't be there with you, we want to let you know about accepted patient positions to consider when deciding how to best position the victim during treatment.

National Safety Council First Aid training recommends the following:

Recovery Position

In an Active Killer Attack in the Hot or Warm Zone, place an unconscious but breathing victim into the recovery position.

The recovery position is one in which you extend the victim's arm above their head and then carefully roll the victim onto their side (same side as the extended arm), allowing the victim's head to be supported by the extended arm.

Bend both legs to help stabilize the victim in this position.

Open the victim's mouth to allow drainage of blood and fluids.

Monitor their breathing. Be ready to do CPR if the scene is secure (Cold Zone).

Shock Position

Responsive victims with no evidence of trauma: you should position the person on their back, and if it does not cause pain you may raise the victim's legs so the feet are 6 - 12 inches off the ground.

Unresponsive victim with no evidence of trauma: you should place the person in the recovery position.

Spinal Motion Restriction

If your victim has a head injury or you suspect a spinal cord injury, initiate the Spinal Motion Restriction position.

Responsive victim:

1. Explain that they need to hold their head still to prevent spinal movement.

2. Hold the victim's head and neck with both hands in the position they were found to prevent movement of the neck and spine.

Unresponsive victim: Hold the victim's head and neck with both hands in the position they were found to prevent movement of the neck and spine. Open the airway with the Jaw Thrust Maneuver.

Continue to hold stabilization until you are able to secure them to a lifting device and extricate them from the scene.

Monitor their breathing and be ready to do CPR.

Putting it all together

1. Identify and treat life-threatening injuries.

2. If caught in an Active Killing, do not run without a plan! Before moving, think ahead on how you will get out. Plan your route of evacuation before proceeding.

3. Follow all police directives. When safe, evacuate the wounded to other first responders or emergency medical services.

4. Give a full report when transferring care to responding EMS and at the ED, especially your treatment and location of all tourniquets.

Remember!

Active Killer / Terrorist attacks can happen anywhere, anytime and to anybody!

Terrorists are using suicide bombers and causing blast injuries to victims around them.

Be on alert to the possibility. They have said they want to cause harm and death to citizens and first responders!

When in a chaotic scene have spotters to watch for potential threats as you help the wounded.

➡This is a new age of violence and we must be hypervigilant!

➡If you see something, say something to the proper authorities.

Chapter 8 Quiz

1. The goal of treating a sucking chest wound is to seal the wound/s immediately.

    True

    False

2. Victims with a sucking chest wound experience extreme shortness of breath and rapid pulse. The lung may collapse.

    True

    False

3. It is not necessary to check for an exit wound when someone is shot in the chest.

    True

    False

4. With victims of a blast if you see singeing or burns to the face, be on high alert for swelling and burns to the upper airway.

True

False

5. If a victim has traumatic amputation of a limb, there is minimal risk of bleeding.

True

False

6. There is usually only one blast, so you don't need to be on high alert for a secondary explosion.

True

False

Chapter Nine

Special considerations for EMS

Warm Zone - EMS

FEMA has issued new recommendations for EMS in active shooter situations.

FEMA highly recommends joint department training with BLS - PD – FD – ALS – First Responders training together to prepare for an Active Shooting situation.

In many states and countries, joint task forces are being formed as services join to work together. It has become clear in the recent attacks that simply staging EMS and not allowing them in to start treatment at the point of wounding is costing lives.

It is important to know what is going on in your state or country as to the current recommendations and available training. We believe that staging alone will be a thing of the past eventually, so it is imperative that everyone in EMS get involved in this early planning and training.

Warm Zone

Normally EMS is staged away from the Hot Zone and not called in until the killer(s) has been neutralized. At this point in history most of us in EMS are not trained to go into the Hot or Warm Zones (only PD goes into Hot Zone), but this is rapidly changing!

New Guidelines from Homeland Security in summary:

New considerations should be made for more aggressive EMS operations in areas of higher but mitigated risk to ensure casualties can be rapidly retrieved, triaged, treated, and evacuated. Rapid triage and treatment are critical to survival.

Understand the difference between cover (protection from direct fire) and concealment (protection from observation).

Remove victims from the danger zone in a manner consistent with predetermined agency training and standards of practice.

LE officers may have to bypass casualties in order to eliminate the threat.

Stage fire/EMS resources, identify, and <u>prepare personnel for operations in areas of higher risk</u>, if appropriate, and await instruction.

Seven Key Points to Consider

1. The staging area should provide hard cover and concealment from perpetrators.

2. Minimize people exposed to unnecessary risk.

3. Provide appropriate protective gear to personnel operating in indirect threat areas.

4. If bystanders become hostile, extricate yourself.

5. Have a "duress code" known to all responder personnel.

6. CCPs should always be considered when providing indirect threat care. Use internal CCPs for large area facilities with multiple casualties where evacuation distances are long.

7. <u>Point-of-wounding medical stabilization should occur prior to evacuation to the CCP. The CCP</u> should provide cover to the injured responders and be secured by LE officers.

<u>Identify people at CCP for accountability and protection of staff.</u>

<u>Warm Zones require LEO escort, and all EMS providers should be issued and wear ballistic body armor.</u>

Chapter 9 ASRT Quiz

1. The Warm Zone is a safe zone.

   True

   False

2. All EMS have been trained for going into the Warm Zone.

   True

   False

3. FEMA has new recommendations for EMS in active shooter situations, including combined department training for BLS - PD – FD – ALS – First Responders.

   True

   False

4. Have a **"duress code"** known to all responder personnel.

   True

   False

Chapter Ten

Training for an Active Shooter/Stabber

If vs. WHEN

You must approach your preparation and training for Active Killer situations, not from a passive "If position," but from the position of "WHEN."

Make training worse than real.

It has been said: "You do not rise to the occasion in combat, you sink to the level of training."

Training for Law Enforcement, Emergency Medical Services and Fire Departments.

Train To Respond, LLC

OSRT: Officer Shot Response Training Course (worth 3 continuing education credits from NJ Dept. of Health)

ASRT: Active Shooter Response Training Course (worth 4 continuing education credits from NJ Dept. of Health)

WRS Security, LLC & Train To Respond, LLC

Rescue Task Force & Tactical Trauma Care (worth 7 continuing education credits from NJ Dept. of Health)

WRS Security, LLC

Rescue Task Force consultation and planning.

Site Security Plans

To schedule training or request a speaker for your event please contact laura@traintorespond.com.

California - Officer Survival Solutions

President & CEO: Marc Barry.

Phone: 760 - 696-0120

email: marc@officersurvivalsolutions.com

Courses & products

Downed Officer Course

Active Shooter Kits

Ballistic Gear

Training for Laypersons
We come to your facility!

Active Threat Survival / Active Shooter Response Training & Tactical Trauma is available for organizations, schools, corporations, gun clubs, and groups.

To schedule a course or request a speaker for your event or group, please contact us at Train To Respond, LLC

email: laura@traintorespond.com or call 973-945-7954.

Visit our website: www.traintorespond.com

Online Bleed Control Specialist Training for family - community - business is available at traintorespond.mykajabi.com

Final Exam RTF & Tactical Trauma Course: Post Test -
50 Questions

RTF Section

1. What is an Active Shooter/Active Killer Event?

   A. Individual(s) actively engaged in killing or attempting to kill people in a confined and populated area.

   B. Individual(s) who enters a building and hurts people.

   C. A mentally ill person who is upset.

   D. A person who is driven by religious beliefs to injury someone.

2. The Rescue Task Force will only deploy at the direction of law enforcement.

   True

   False

3. What is a Rescue Task Force?

A. A team of highly trained medical providers who provide advance medical care.

B. A team of first responders who provide medical support to a SWAT Team.

C. A task force that combines the resources of volunteers from the Fire and EMS Services for immediate deployment at the direction of local law enforcement to Active Shooter/Active Killer incidents.

D. All of the above

4. A Rescue Task Force is designed to operate in:

A. The Hot Zone - area where there is immediate danger.

B. The Cold Zone - area where little danger exists.

C. The Warm Zone - area where danger is possible.

D. The Green Zone - area secured by law enforcement.

5. In 2014 and 2015, _____was the fourth leading cause of fatal occupational injuries in the United States.

A. Motor Vehicles Accidents

B. Fire

C. Homicide

D. Cancer

6. The majority of Active Shooter/ Active Killer Events last more than 15 minutes.

True

False

7. Approximately 40% of Active Shooter/Active Killer events involve more than one offender.

True

False

8. Active Shooter/Active Killer events are the sole responsibility of law enforcement?

True

False

9. More than 50% of the Active Shooter/Active Killer events have taken place in schools.

True

False

10. Less than 10% of Active Shooter / Active Killer Events are over before the arrival of law enforcement.

True

False

11. The Rescue Task Force is never allowed to move a patient until a patient assessment has been completed and all injuries have been treated.

True

False

12._____ are concerns for first responders during an Active Shooter/Active Killer event.

A. Firearms

B. Explosives

C. Fire as a weapon

D. Knives

E. All of the above

13. Approximately 80% of Active Shooter/Active Killer Events are Mass Casualty Incidents.

True

False

14. Direct Threat Care involves all of the following except:

A. Tourniquet

B. Direct Pressure

C. Recovery Position

D. Splinting

15. Law Enforcement operating in the Hot Zone will conduct triage consisting of the following conditions:

A. Red, Yellow and Green

B. Red, Green, Yellow and Black

C. Red and Green

D. Black, Blue, Red and Green

16. When deciding on a Casualty Collection Point (CCP), the following should be considered with the exception of:

A. Location

B. Size

C. Presence of smoke detectors

D. Defensible location

17. The Rescue Task Force should never be concerned with hypothermia when treating a patient.

True

False

18. The Casualty Collection Point can never be established within the Warm Zone.

True

False

19. All first responders should be trained in "self-aid."

True

False

20. One of the best strategies to protect yourself during an Active Shooter/Active Killer event is:

A. Run fast and far.

B. Never run in a straight line.

C. Avoid, Deny, Defend, Survive.

D. Hide and Hope or Play Dead.

21. While operating in the Hot Zone, members of the Rescue Task Force should insert an Oral Airway into all Casualties before moving them.

True

False

22. The difference between utilizing cover vs. concealment in a threat environment is that concealment provides responders some level of ballistic protection.

True

False

23. A hallway should always be a primary consideration for a Casualty Collection Point.

    True

    False

24. Ideally, the Rescue Task Force staff shall team up with their law enforcement security element _____

    A. At the entry point

    B. Inside the CCP

    C. Inside the building

    D. At the staging area

25. The Ambulance Exchange Point can be located in the Hot Zone as long as the RTF has a Security Element.

    True

    False

Tactical Trauma Section

Fill in the blank & Essay

26. List the three types of bleeding.

   1.

   2.

   3.

27. _____ bleeding will kill you within 3 - 5 minutes if not treated.

28. List three ways to control bleeding.

   1.

   2.

   3.

29. You are an off-duty first responder in an area where a rescue task force is in place. You are aiding an officer down. The task force arrives with paramedics and EMTs who are able to get to where you are. What should you tell them about this injured officer?

30. Define self aid:

31. Define buddy aid:

32. Provide reasons as to why a tourniquet needs to be kept on your person and not in the emergency vehicle or first aid kit.

Multiple Choice

33. Venous bleeding is NOT:

A. Slow and steady flow.

B. Dark red in color.

C. Spurting out with each beat of the heart.

34. When you apply a tourniquet you should tell EMS/Trauma Team the following:

A. Time you placed tourniquet on.

B. Location of tourniquet.

C. Why you applied a tourniquet.

D. All of the above.

35. What critical items should be included in an Active Shooter kit:

A. Tourniquet.

B. Pressure bandage.

C. Hemostatic gauze or agent.

D. PPE - gloves.

E. All of the above.

36. During **the first phase** of care under fire you should:

A. Move yourself or victim to area of cover and stop arterial bleeding.

B. If no pulse is felt - begin CPR.

C. Buddy aid a victim in respiratory arrest by ventilating them.

37. You arrive at a domestic in progress. While approaching the front door of the residence, shots ring out, and you watch your partner fall to the ground. Your partner is bleeding heavily from the left leg and begins to panic. You should:

A. Panic with him.

B. Rush into the line of fire to rescue your partner.

C. Instruct your partner to apply the tourniquet he is carrying.

38. You are finally able to reach your partner and get him to an area of cover. You reassess the GSW to his leg and notice it is still bleeding quite heavily. You should:

A. Immediately apply direct pressure to the wound.

B. Apply a second tourniquet above the first and tighten until bleeding stops.

C. If bleeding still does not stop and you carry hemostatic gauze, open the packet and push it into the wound until it touches the bleeding artery and hold pressure.

D. All of the above.

39. After stopping the bleeding you notice your partner is having difficulty breathing, and when you reach out to steady him, you feel his shirt is drenched with sticky wetness. You suspect:

A. Nosebleed.

B. Sucking chest wound.

C. He's sweating.

40. Because you suspect a sucking chest wound, you should immediately.

A. Remove his shirt and if possible keep his vest on, as you assess the area.

B. Look for both an entrance and an exit wound.

C. Immediately cover all wounds with a chest seal.

D. All of the above.

41. The scene is now declared safe by police. As you are moving to the rig, your partner stops breathing. You should:

A. Rush him into the rig.

B. Start ventilations using a bag value mask or barrier device.

C. Cease all efforts.

True or False

42. All EMS are part of a rescue task force that will respond into the Warm Zone at an active shooting or stabbing event?

True

False

43. You can easily spot an arterial bleed, even through dark clothing.

    True

    False

44. You should keep your active shooter kit with you at all times when on duty.

    True

    False

45. A sucking chest wound does not need to be sealed to prevent air going into the chest.

    True

    False

46. You should hold pressure on the hemostatic gauze for 1 minute.

    True

    False

47. This test is pretty long and you are really glad it's almost over!

   True

   False

48. The most common cause of death from a survivable gunshot/stab wound is the failure to rapidly apply a tourniquet.

   True

   False

49. One of the most important things you can do to avoid a terror truck or car attack is to be aware of your surroundings at all times.

   True

   False

50. Tactical Trauma Training is proven to save lives.

   True

   False

End Exam

Practice Scenarios

General use

Scenario 1

You are in a meeting and suddenly you hear screaming and a crowd of co-workers is running towards you. Shots ring out behind them and you watch as several fall to the ground. What are your survival options? What is your plan?

Scenario 2

While attending an office party two co-workers suddenly start fighting. One of the men pulls out a knife and stabs the other in the chest. The perpetrator flees the scene, leaving the knife sticking out of the second man's chest. The victim grabs his chest, stumbles and collapses to the ground.

Scenario 3

You are out with your family eating at a local restaurant. Outside you hear gunshots ring out and people screaming. What steps do you take to help yourself and your family survive?

EMS

Scenario 1

You are dispatched on a routine shortness of breath call at a well-known address. The man living there has always been okay with EMS, but seems to hate the police.

You pull up behind the police cruiser and notice the lights are on and the driver's door is open. As you step out of the rig, you glance down and see the responding police officer unconscious on the ground.

Bright red blood is pooling around his upper body and you can't see where it is coming from. He still is breathing and has a pulse.

EMS

<u>Scenario 2</u>

You are dispatched to the ten-plex movie theater for a man outside bleeding. You pull up behind the first arriving police officer and hear shots coming from inside the theater. The man initially called for is surrounded by a pool of blood and is not moving. Crowds of people are dashing out the doors and running across the parking lot. Shots ring out inside and a police officer radios he's hit. A police officer hands you a bulletproof vest and requests you enter the scene with him carrying your Active Shooter response bag.

Upon entering the lobby you see several people down.

Patient 1: GSW to the head. Not breathing.

Patient 2: GSW to the upper arm. Bright red blood is spurting out and pooling around her as she sits, leaning against the snack counter.

Patient 3: Walking with a dazed look and a cut to his nose he says he got when he tripped and fell.

Patient 4: Young male lying supine not moving. As you do a quick look-over, you notice a darkening spot on the lower part of his jean-covered leg that seems to be growing bigger.

LEO

Scenario 1

You and your partner respond to a report of an open door of a residence. You take the front, and your partner goes to the back. As you near the front door, you hear a shot. Your partner radios he's been shot. You find him on the ground barely conscious. You reach down, touching his leg, and come up with a hand covered with bright red blood.

Scenario 2

Dispatched to a husband and wife domestic, you arrive on scene and get out of your cruiser. You are immediately confronted and shot in the upper arm by the husband. As other units arrive, the husband runs away and you drop to the ground holding your arm.

Resources

FEMA Is - 907 - Active Shooter: What you can do.

https://emilms.fema.gov/IS907/ASo1.

<u>You Tube</u>

Arterial Bleeding - leg: the dexitvideo.

Could you take 3 shots to the chest: The Smithsonian Channel.

Ready Houston - Run - Hide - Fight - Surviving an active shooter event.

Avoid Deny Defend - at www.avoiddenydefend.org.

Conclusion

Thank you for investing in yourself, your family, friends, co-workers and the future of our world.

Together we can make a difference and empower ourselves and others when confronted with acts of violence and terrorism.

Until we meet again, remember to always be aware of your surroundings. If you see something or your gut tells you something is wrong, then say something to the proper authorities.

To be better prepared, it is imperative you get in-person Active Shooter Response Training and Tactical Trauma Care with live scenarios so you will feel better able to handle the critical situations mentioned in this book. Training is everything!

Peace

Laura & Bill

Works cited

1. "First Responder Guide for Improving Survivability in Improvised Explosive Device and/or Active Shooter Incidents." Homeland Security, Office of Health Affairs, June 2015.

2. "Active Shooter Preparedness." Homeland Security. www.dhs.gov/active-shooter-preparedness

3. *Mass Shooting Tracker.* This site counts the number of people shot rather than only the number killed and is updated as shootings happen. www.shootingtracker.com

4. Henriques Jasmine. "Mass Shootings in America: A Historical Review." *Global Research News,* June 13, 2016.

5. "Avoid/ Deny/ Defend." *ALERRT Center at Texas State University.* http://www.avoiddenydefend.org

6. "DOL Workplace Violence Program." *U.S. Department of Lab*

7. "Workplace Violence Fact Sheet." OSHA.

8. "Improving Active Shooter / Hostile Event Response." (September 2015). *InterAgency Board,* September, 2015

9. "The Hartford Consensus III: Implementation of Bleeding Control Joint Committee to Create a National Policy to Enhance

Survivability from Intentional Mass-Casualty and Active Shooter Events." (2015). *Bulletin of The American College of Surgeons*.

10. "Department Operational Considerations and Guide for Active Shooter and Mass Casualty Incidents." United States Department of Homeland Security-U.S. Fire Administration Fire/Emergency Medical Service, September 2013.

11. "Local, State and Federal Standardization and Interoperability Report- Improving Active Shooter / Hostile Event Response- Best Practice Recommendations for Integrating Law Enforcement, Fire, and EMS." September 2015.

12. "First Responder Guide for Improving Survivability in Improvised Explosive Device and/or Active Shooter Incidents." *Office of Health Affairs, United States Department of Homeland Security*, June 2015.

13. "Planning and Response to an Active Shooter: An Interagency Security Committee Policy and Best Practice Guide." *United States Department of Homeland Security*.

14. "EMS in the Warm Zone Active Shooter Best Practice Guide." *New Hampshire Bureau of EMS*, 2015.

15. "Study of Active Shooter Incidents in the United States Between 2000 and 2013." The United States Department of Justice, Federal Bureau of Investigations

16. Activate Threat Integrated Response Training (ATIR/PER-340). *United States Department of Homeland Security.*

17. "Active Shooter Incident Management (ASIM/PER-353)." *United States Department of Homeland Security.*

18. ALERRT: Texas State University Terrorism Response Tactics Active Shooter Training. 2011. http://www.ct.gov/post/lib/post/course_outline/active_shooter_re sponse_training.pdf

19. "Active Shooter Event Quick Reference Guide." *United States Department of Homeland Security.*

20. "U.S. Fire Administration Guide for Fire/Emergency Medical Service Department Operational Considerations and Guide for Active Shooter and Mass Casualty Incident." *United States Department of Homeland Security,* September 2013.

21. Blair, P & Schweit, K. W. (2014). *A Study of Active Shooter Incidents, 2000-2013.* Washington D.C.; Texas State University, Federal Bureau of Investigation and U.S. Department of Justice.

22. "ICS 100 and ICS 200.Department of Homeland Security, FEMA, 2004.

23. Godfrey, W., Agen D., Otterbacher, R., and Fender, D., "Active Shooter Incident Management Checklist." *C3 Pathways*, 2014. https://www.c3pathways.com/acs/Active_Shooter_Checklist_Help_Guide_pdf.

24. "Firearms and Explosives- Bomb Threat Stand Off Chart." The United States Department of Homeland Security, Bureau of Alcohol, Tobacco and Firearms.

Appendix

Pretest Answer Key

1. A.

2. C.

3. C.

4. C.

5. E.

6. F.

7. C.

8. D.

9. E.

10. F.

11. F.

12. T.

13. F.

14. F.

15. F.

16. F.

17. F.

Quiz Answer Keys

Chapter 1 Quiz

1. False.

2. True.

3. True.

Chapter 2. Quiz

1. False.

2. False.

3. True.

Chapter 3 Quiz

1. True.

2. False.

3. True.

4. True.

Chapter 4 Quiz

1. True.

2. False.

3. Hot Zone.

4. Warm Zone.

5. True.

Chapter 5 Quiz

1.A. Avoid.

B. Deny.

C. Defend.

2. False

3. Cover: is an object or objects that are likely to stop bullets.

Concealment: Basically not being seen. Offers no ballistic protection.

Chapter 6 Quiz

1. False.
2. B.

3. False.

Chapter 7 Quiz

1. True.

2. C.

3. False.

4. False.

5. C.

6. False.

Chapter 8 Quiz

1. True.

2. True.

3. False.

4. True.

5. False.

6. False.

Chapter 9 Quiz

1. False.

2. False.

3. True.

4. True.

Final Exam Answer Key

1. A.
2. T.
3. C.
4. C.
5. C.
6. F.
7. F.
8. F.
9. F.
10. F.
11. F.
12. E.
13. F.
14. D
15. C.
16. C.
17. F.
18. F.
19. T.
20. C.
21. F.
22. F.
23. F.
24. D.

25. F.

26. Arterial, Venous, Capillary.

27. Arterial

28. Direct Pressure, Tourniquet, Hemostatic Gauze, Pressure Bandage.

29. Report what happened to the officer, injuries you found on your RTA and treatment provided - especially the location of all tourniquets and time applied.

30. Self Aid: Treatment you do to save your own life.

31. Buddy Aid: Treatment you do to save another person's life. (This may also mean instructing others how to aid themselves if you are unable to reach them.

32. Because by the time you get to your vehicle or get out your first aid / trauma kit you will be too weak to help yourself or will already have bled to death.

33. C.

34. D.

35. E.

36. A.

37. C.

38. D.

39. B.

40. D.

41. B.

42. F.

43. F.

44. T.

45. F.

46. F. (3 minutes.)

47. T.

48. T.

49. T.

50. T

NOTES

Made in the USA
Middletown, DE
02 April 2018